My Baptism Day!

Written and Illustrated by
Madeline Parrish

Dedication

Dedicated to my parents and all those who
instilled in me a love of the sacraments

About the Author

Madeline Parrish resides in Cumberland RI with her husband and two daughters. She enjoys staying home full time with her children, baking, watercolor painting, and finding beauty in the present moment. A lover of the sacraments, she hopes to enrich her readers with this charming Baptism book.

My Baptism day
starts my friendship with the Lord.
He brings me Himself, my soul He
restores.

On my soul, Jesus places His mark.
My faith is ignited from this first glorious
spark.

DIVINE
MERCY

Original sin is completely wiped away.
Sacramental grace, here in me to stay.

Clothed in a garment of white,
it represents my clean soul,
Full of Christ's light.

Totus
Tuus

Jesus now resides in my heart.
My soul is given a fresh new start.

WELCOME TO
THE CHURCH!

The Body of Christ welcomes me in
because Jesus Christ has renewed me within.

Now I'm a Catholic
For as long as I live.
I'll learn to listen, to love, and to always
forgive.

In Baptism, God gives us beautiful gifts...
A clean soul, godparents, and sacramental
grace
Heart wide open we receive His
loving embrace.

Question

1. Why are we "clothed in a garment of white" at Baptism?

"The white garment symbolises that the person baptised has 'put on Christ', has risen with Christ." (*Catechism of the Catholic Church, #1243*). It shows our purity as our sins are washed away.

Question

2. What is the purpose of godparents?

The purpose of godparents is to help the child grow in their practice of the faith. They should model a Catholic life, support the parents, and represent the Church. The Catechism of the Catholic Church states that "godparents should be firm believers who are able and ready to help the baptized" (Catechism of the Catholic Church, #1255)

Question

3. On page 12, the text reads, "the body of Christ welcomes me in". What is "Body of Christ" referring to here?

The *Catholic Church!* *The Catholic Church* is also known as the Mystical Body of Christ.

Question

4. What are the other 6 sacraments in the *Catholic Church?*

Reconciliation Holy Communion Confirmation Matrimony Anointing of the Sick Holy Orders.